A Reaction to Someone Coming In

FUTUREPOEM BOOKS
NEW YORK CITY
2023

A Reaction to Someone Coming In

Wendy Lotterman

first edition | first printing

This edition first published in paperback by Futurepoem
P.O. Box 7687 JAF Station
NY, NY 10116
www.futurepoem.com

Executive Editor: Dan Machlin
Managing Editor: Aiden Farrell
Associate Editor & futurefeed Editor: Ariel Yelen
Assistant Editor & Submissions Coordinator: Ahana Ganguly
Guest Editors: Hannah Black, Ken Chen, and Mónica de la Torre
Cover design: Everything Studio (www.everythingstudio.com)
Interior design: HR Hegnauer (www.hrhegnauer.com)
Copyeditor: Liv Schwenk
Typeface: Garamond, Tw Cen MT
Printed in the United States of America on acid-free paper

This project is supported by awards from the National Endowment for the Arts, the New York State Council on the Arts with the support of Governor Kathy Hochul and the New York State Legislature, and by public funds from the New York City Department of Cultural Affairs in partnership with the City Council. Futurepoem is also supported by our individual donors, subscribers, and readers, The Literary Arts Emergency Fund, Tamaas, Leslie Scalapino Fund, New York Community Trust, and Leaves of Grass Fund. Futurepoem Inc. is a New York state-based 501(c)3 non-profit organization dedicated to creating a greater public awareness and appreciation of innovative literature.

Distributed to the trade by Small Press Distribution, Berkeley, California
Toll-free number (U.S. only): 800.869.7553
Bay Area/International: 510.524.1668
orders@spdbooks.org
www.spdbooks.org

CONTENTS

A REACTION
TO SOMEONE
COMING IN

THE IMPRECISION OF GROUPS

Lifted up by blonds and the comic victory of the particular, like the city and my mom in a fake, spontaneous duet. The financial district falls into her lap so that no good thing can be saved from a three-legged relay with the bad. Layers of grudge and wonder collapse into a single, unsalted cracker while miles of superstitious sun signs combust in a triangle of fire with liquor and wet-wipes. Reggie curls into ringlets of love and disgust, nestling in settlements of incest and redness at the heart of his own sterile starfish. Neither ass nor mouth is undone by the circumference of the other, but the bedtimes of both get stretched by nights of progressively wider size, an axis of appetite wrapped in plastic and dipped in Teflon honey. Awakened by the displaced taste of inverted cane, you realize anxiety always rides before the reason it is anxious to erase. Laws and observation lock inverted lips like Charlie's chocolate ancestors in the single, king-sized bed. Golden favors. A Mr. Clean eraser. A circle of dirt and sanitation in which each outruns the other at the exact same pace. Early attempts to tuck the chin as you dive leave you blind to the alliance of dexterity and class. Money and sunscreen make the body spontaneously align, as displaced volumes of water speak inverse volumes of the body's native grace. Somewhere in the middle of all of this is a timeline of fungible love in which I forgot to say that I couldn't come home on half-days to find the light of two perverted suns doing sex things on the bed, since the golf-balls in my wallet cannot feel or be felt. Topical fondants take new names when the tips are black or frosted, so the flaxen are outed by the only sexed adjective in English, getting off beneath screens of mesh and jean, left with the disharmonic gloss of an improvised, neon costume and the generic heather jersey of the Colorado Rockies. Riding that wave, not the cool synthetic scoreboard of moral proxies, I avoid the challenge. To live one way or another. Escaping from the shade inside that one maternal cubby and the secrets of its warm performance fleece, I draw two blond sons in the analyst's second-hand dollhouse, resurrecting the waxy grave of dispossessed yellows and a single-track message from my parents. That it will be okay; that this genealogical contract cannot be renewed. Two cousins. Corn rows. Code words hidden in the post-cards. In the woods we measure the circumference of recessive reds and cry beneath the shade of a camo Abercrombie visor. Jackie says her nipples are the smallest in a competition to which no one consented. Smears of ejected chicken tenders and wood pulp are an end-rhyme with the fireworks of the first official social. Duets of cream and sunscreen. Your wrist writes the sequel: the classic khaki braid of rich Nantucket bracelets. These details go dormant in the winter as other kinds of release are sustained in the shape of vacant upstate cabins, where butts butt heads with head and jump through hoops of softened Swiss cheese. Eggs on the underside of a frying pan, a brain lit up by the unseasonal desire for more life than any life can give. Now and then, portraits of young girls present two alternative futures in which I accept either the meltdown of mountaintop removal, or the secondary embellishments of Jello. Each infertile world waits just beyond the path of greatest pleasure, indefensible against the path of least disgrace. Parental love is enormous and mistakenly cast as the foil to all future partners. The jury admits to this: duets of Gatorade and shame; a miscarriage of flowers in the garden. Dancing with that one particular star is the unchecked patient-zero of all successive tingles on the warm, embroidered scoreboard of the emerald, velvet loveseat. I cover the airspace with my grandma's checkered afghan, swapping one profanity for another, weaving secrets, which I pay to reveal. On another couch, I confess to jealousies that won't leave the session. Tonight is different from all other nights. But there is a reason that the question is asked so many times, even if it is obvious why we dip twice, and why you and I choose to recline.

FOIL

I ordered a comb in toile that hasn't come

Or got lost between several addresses,

None of which is completely accurate.

Scenes of service mix ahistorically

With luxury and fawns. The claws

Rake her hair into aisles of seed –

No framework or felon could extract

The monastic plot of that garden.

Fishing for tines, aligned like angels

On an illegally bifurcated pinhead.

Why consent to live in images,

The picture already populated by

So many iterations of a single tremulous day?

But this isn't a story of privation.

Beset by a mild discomfort that radiates

Like bangs around an unfamiliar head.

That it belongs to all of us, like a

Risky psychic timeshare, cannot be undone

By exit, or speech act, or law.

I wanted to talk.

The fog abandoned the treetops.

Something was off in the air pressure–

Jaws felt locked and the topic was beyond

What was possible to talk about.

You wish for company to revive the

Part that a certain tap shut off, but

Nobody, not even kids, can join

The cast as water. No one can be blamed

If the message was wrong from the start, but the

Image depicted in the ruffle of reused aluminum

Gives us something to warn against,

Like Oedipus or Orestes or siblings.

Let us rob them. When this family
Is discovered to be the secret of that
Family, it is difficult to keep. Up in
The steam room, nursed by
Noise and heat, the faucet talks
Down tapestries of scenes telling
Something other than stories. Trial
By lyre, lying bilateral fires in a
Race-car twin-sized coincidence.
Winded by ten strokes of butterfly.
I don't remember anything of the

Room. The event postdates the mood
It turned into. Agree, from here on,
To proceed down court without feet.
Floored by hands and extremely
Good reasons for being here. Missed
The meet. Met again by the museum,

On steps of gifts and grass. The
Best thing about my birthday is yours.
Weeks go by like strokes of fat on
Glass in heat, greased for ejection
In one piece. The open field opens

Its ear for you. One finger remains
Cautiously on the game piece, but
We leave before learning that the
Resemblance has several accepted
Spellings. Light speaks in threes.
Love infests the brain like seedless
Melon. In June, the gems are neither
House nor guest, but a reaction to
Someone coming in. Let them rob us,
And us them. The mold breeds weakly,
Like the roof was only ever a suggestion.

The spectrum from

She to y'all fails to account for

The narrowness of patrimony,

Talking in tangles to The Hague between

Highly localized parades,

As if only the specificity of this pasture

Could make that milk,

And only this cave could taste like

The lack of that particular sky.

Cake and lotus line the aisle to a hazy destination.

In your language, which is not quite mine,

All these obsessions are wrong.

But the smell bursts right through the hallway

And I am called to the door by something

Other than knowledge.

Depressions gather debris from

Fleeting scenes, some trash hanging back like

The serendipitous invention of dogs.

In this case, the subtype inherited

Too much sleep and a habit of licking persistently.

On one throne, the comfort of a comfort

Shoved slightly up the nose. On the other,

The baroqueness of constraint,

Making a case for the intricacy of shame.

Only whispers can contain the

Painful decorousness of this truth,

Repeating the twists of its entrance

With emphasis as it moves in reverse.

The scene does not belong to any room,

Or bed, or season of reality, propped

On boxes of unused standard gloss.

No access, holy or vernacular,

Could really capture that atmosphere,

So the signal has to do something else.

The shelves are named Billy, the dog is not mine.

Guests threaten on levels I can't defend.

Details escape the record,

Which is not a euphemism,

But a very high floor downtown.

FAULT STATS

The search for local trash and
Conference cheese as meals reveal
Something wrong with the water:
A conveyance across bisected
Lifestyles that split between the banks.
Stettin Venice floats as fictive sky
Beyond the fruit flies. Linked by limbs
To the losing end of a charitable simile–
The street is like weed, the weeds are like
Ideas leading further away from the
Monument, erect at the center of a
Concept turned fragile that bends and
Bursts in the off season. No one can
Decide whether roads are the problem,
Even if they lead us out. A package at
The doorstep contains more than
Its contents, a basket that blows out
The address. At the risk of being lost

Or turned to salt, the message reads

One of two ways: Don't turn around, or:

Angel, I don't think I c am come this week.

GLIDERS

I had them play tag in the background,

Diving for dollars in a mechanically inorganic

Dunk-tank; the watermelon dropped,

Not in competition with a feather,

But to enumerate the uses of fruit.

The capacity to hide or hit nails

Hovers over the daffodils, not knowing their

Own readiness to activate a dilapidated flashpoint.

Bee stings come and go. The doctrine of

Discovery is responsible for the racetrack,

Where icons float like monarchs toward a

Flashy Vegas payout. Blaming

The dog for the day, the dark for the night,

All the arrows point directly to a single

Persistent strobe that hides love

In perforations of daylight.

There's no such thing as a splash that

emancipates from the bath.

The struggle to be calm on Halloween

Comes from the hoax of an unnamed ubiquity

That punctuates the ghost like

A spectral phallic talisman.

Night is soothed by the imprecision of groups.

Ouija pools the riddle into unison.

The community garden is not only a solution

But a smock atop the scandal of psychology.

Something got stuck inside the blow-up planetarium,

Adopted by a nylon rip-stop rainbow that

Trapped us, shapeless, with the wind

during gym class. Why that particular floral silk

Felt so full of life on the bike ride,

So ready to confess the secret of a feminine

Investment, is kneaded with the seasons,

Preserved in a resin that evenly splits the difference.

The bull will hold onto itself this time,

Bucking nothing but the painful swivel

Of repertory step-work.

INTENSE HOLIDAY

FAMILY TRIAGE

I put my life on the fridge with a chip-clip,
covering the corrugated skin of a much bigger face
or a fever too hot not to know we got it wrong.

The red keppie backpedals regret into a belated
amnio waiting room. I paint the nursery yellow
to cover my own advanced knowledge. I return to

the race once the ribbon breaks. The world-lap
stands up. Once you go back, you never go back.
Perhaps we got it wrong. Perhaps the baby and

the bathwater switched places while we were
getting tucked into a comfier sensorium. Urgencies
confer in a handshake; the face card lays down

and wins the race. Whatever happens, I still love you
in the soft-core ectopic bedroom the time zones
consensually remember. Even now, as panic

reanimates from the whiplash of unlimited forecast.
In ways I don't need to rank anything, least of all
my care; in other ways my mom will always come

first, since kids are the future and that gift cannot
be ungiven, even if I take it. Coherence mistakenly
relies on the trick-ribbon of originary presence

and its reproduction beyond the subject it delivers.
You get less endless and something else endures.
I get on the couch with no intention to be legible.

And yet, some kind of centrism straps me down,
and contamination phobia plays out like an expensive,
invisible fence. The dogs just sunbathe alone.

It isn't enough, especially when the literal division
of space means some histories get wetter than
others, making the drought into a chicken and

the war into an oversexed egg, reproducing before
it has even come of age. I lie down on the deck
and wonder why the snow collected just to

force itself back into the cinema of my closeted
attention. The avalanche is Bunnicula, and gas
is such a terrifying state, a tricked-out childhood

antonym of the nebulizer in my bedroom on
repeat. I get on the sofa, not the psychodynamic
melon toss of a trillion hot pink halos collapsing

on the beanbag of my heart, but you, in total
open access. The centerfold cannot hold. I bite
my cup and run both hands across the holistic

lips at the porn awards. Every angelic future
tunes into the solutions embraced on the rightful
froth of your licit Costco screen. The class ghost

goes to bed. My sovereign hand approaches the
table, then slows to pull your hair behind your ear.
Claudia mixes cream into the mashed potatoes

and I politely decline to eat tonight. The accidental
protest isn't my daughter, but the peak inventory
of everything I couldn't say was coming. In some

ways I did this. In other ways I can't be so proud.
It's snowing on my face. No more arms, just a loving,
tentacular conclusion before its normative proof.

You were eating prawns and reading about nonexhaustive love by the pillar in the basement; interrupting the original, like tape on your face or a footbridge you might learn to live for, no sequence too sticky to lift you and leave you where your friend said her dad said there was always a reason for timing. Sleepy or unencumbered, the tan-line moves without you. Events turn your will into a school-issued uniform, neither good nor bad. Bald Britney arrives late to the ball, making reasons for what cannot be choice, which is the unimpeachable avatar of choice, buffering on the resin offset by everything you kept below the jury's official meniscus. I ask only that you please keep your love shut, or go home as you came minus a head full of braids and shame in the key of rosacea. Anguilla quits before the dye sets. The bugs leave your pillow inexplicably wet. That porcelain doll is not a proxy for love, but the shape of its safer translation. Parts of the night return with a different type of wrist as your hand flags the wall, which isn't a limit, but a bell, signaling dinner will be in ten minutes. It's crazy how the cursor can come in or out of view, depending on who else can see the screen. The bodily cognate of mice, offset by earlier keyboards of meaning, like the jets just turn on and do not stop until you put that life to sleep, making action de facto, and painful the effort to refrain. I do understand; that the room just sort of twists and retreats, disappearing into a less intimate cinema of distance. I do understand; if the keyboard hums, move away. Beside the convenience this affords when attempting to eat the pork-chop your roommate prepares after the reading, beside the unheavenly bodies of pop heaved with ease inside the academic test-drive. The reason to choose is removable, like seasonal decals on the kindergarten window. You peel off the turkey. You leave no trace. By morning, things aren't quite sticky enough to create an abscess of immortality on the log where Baby falls, but doesn't fall, and the cabanas revert to homes I learn to treat with permanence. There is a stage at which the world empties out every proper noun, and you, specifically you, sub-in as the tailored fulfillment of what life would like to bat next. I imagine bringing you to temple, were I ever to go. More likely I'd take you to the pool at Autumn Ridge where we'd consign our safety to the lips of a teenager studying for the SATs, white streaks across the palms hugging flotational foam above a less expressive lap. I imagine a trip to Grove where those two years scurry back through a perfect reversal of what was taken and what was shamed, redeeming my sexless teens before we go up the mountains where I've never been, but where Baby inaugurated the modular dream of intimacy on lateral trees. I imagine you in the Catskills. White tea is just black tea that is a baby; green olives are black olives that reach your mouth before their own maturation. However you intend to harvest this now or in a practically revisionary future, I know this baby passed away before it learned how to talk. I want you to know it just as I do, but the one scene I never quite understood involved Baby's dad performing an abortion in an inexplicit room, which I found very haunting, and looked forward to with the same inverted dread I felt when Kirsty Alley dangles from the hand of her literalized biological clock, threatening her grip as it ticks. I imagine things now that give me the feeling those movies gave me then, and then put you in the room, and then feel instantly more comfortable. Most of the early fantasies begin with a very normal public space that gets really full and anonymous, and then, by way of this, we are forced into a closeness at first incidental that then, through a silent but explicit agreement, increasingly fills with intent, like when, after a generally amiable night, five friends try to fit in a cab with four seats, and, because I'm more compact and you casually offer, I sit on your lap where shapes thus far unspoken take place. Then I find you. Then I really find you, next to the pastries and then everywhere, in places insanely native to themselves. Beginning innocent like the puka on your ankle, or flashcards; practicing mnemonics with mom before the quiz pops harder than I have ever seen. I domesticate the reflex to do it again. Fear of what refrain will not repeat, or will repeat, or what the cards cannot help you recover, like a night that encodes as a life but walks out as a night. The phone does not reflect your hand, nor does the other phone that takes a picture of yours taking it back. Dispense the matte affect immediately. It doesn't get how much I'd like to see the psychic dog advisor, so long as he is you. You were reading patience without something to wait for. Breaking faith in the zipper of your jeans, making natural detractors of those who had no reason to be there. The mouse in the keyboard is an interstitial exit between letters, except when it is what it represents: that the ThinkPad's clitoral contact can be depicted as an accident between "H" and "G." We agree, it is better when the parasites do not study you back. To the one who sits on my feet I say: if the worst thing in the world is that good things are better without you, I can't operate on my child in the morning. Shiba wants to know if I'm good. She asks me to revert to her by night with a positive response and statistics on how she can assist me. I am tempted to read meaning in coincidence. Pizza flies off into my room the same day I refuse to go near it. The crush slips like Teflon the day it's brought to term. On the other hand, those walls were there for you, uncommon to any secondary moxie that could force its stock before or after dinner. The lightness of a punch you kept for the secret to stay open, advanced beyond any objection and all reactive hospitality that might collapse the space cleared for a face that I was already making. But then I made a new one. Choice is not the bodily cognate of desire, but occasionally what it needs to be. A lightly feathered cube rubs off when you touch it, so you find other ways to keep it close. There is no other option. When I ask you to prop my chin and you do, there is no other option. This much you could have intuited, but that intuition required every effort it took to get there. That life is too busy having fun to sit still for a picture is what happens before it's pulled off the bush. That I didn't think to take any, or even one, since this house goes on forever from the inside. I wake up unconvinced that there are lobsters in any other garden. For one thing, people come in very different ways. Plus, your pulse can't take the pulse of mine as it is taking you back. The choice to feel good arrives this time without an alternative, at which point I struggle to say how many stars I would give Convivium Osteria, in part because my father arrived one hour late, and I was busy debriding leaves from Elijah's empty seat. When he got there, I told him. I couldn't help it. The psychic dog kept spiking my temperature. There are other ways to say this. Parts of the night return by optimism, or a different brand of seltzer tipped onto the moods you would like to retrieve. Candles are not the vapes of literature; Sbarro will never get the Jewish vote. The curtains freeze immediately for two sets of knees at first perpendicular, then parallel, then irrelevant to space when the sparrow erratic task of the transfer comes home. The weekend is an anagram we end with a reflex to agita in the discretion that surrounds. Wake up as a hand on my back. Take it off before the wires get crossed beneath your office in what is too much now but will not be enough; the real apparent value of a life to be treated with respect, and the fictive adherence to another that hides the shape of what it's missing. The room now breathes as both pairs of knees. What it means is a footnote to what is or can be seen. But of course, other rooms go on forever from the inside, and of course they belong to other people. That house didn't ask to be taken off the beach. It is enough now.

CRUSH

On line for the bathroom at Crush
I dissimulate the vibe and learn that Hannah
absolutely loves the ground. There's an invitation to
my name at the roundabout of your hip. A catalogue
of love gets stored in the blank space of several mesh
jerseys, which is all that you wear for this rainy,
three-day mood ring. I go home in one with
a message redirecting me back to Dublin above
two nylon zeros that contain an extreme willingness
to evaporate the mantle. At this point
I'm pretty sure it doesn't matter
how the mnemonic is spelled.
The investment is temporary.
The importance is more than historic.
Hustle out of the sun for a minute, but please
remember to want to come back.

Cool spots divide in trypophobic protest

on the floor of your sexual preference.

I don't totally know what to say. I'm kept up by

fatigue and a memory of not saying it right.

The altitude of some beds suggests nothing more

than an intrepid ring around the double wide.

Your shorts suggest an altitude of interest. In the

background, asthma attacks at dawn,

leaving the sex toy to wake up as a gummy

LIVESTRONG bracelet.

Confuse the bracelet for yourself,

then leave it on the nightstand.

Some summers ghostwrite the blueprint

of all desire to follow, leaving you to lie, toss the

album, and rearrange the furniture.

Kids gather to make mac 'n' cheese in the garden,

untangling the minted, pubescent demo-kit.

Of course, you wouldn't send your kid to camp

if the mascots were addicts, known to détourn

their own recently detoxed benevolence,

ushering Wendy to the edge of a bed

I can barely remember, chaperoning

intimacy to the speed of its knees,

kissing the floor of unshorn erotic proportions,

where two counselors tighten the seat of a

swivel-chair, mouthing over, beneath,

and between. Four disordered Winds spin

a replica of daytime, sending mom to retract me,

mid-bar-mitzvah, in the silver Mercury wagon.

The two-ply wing of my visual field projects

a crush not brought to term; a dusky, Nike-lined

block where it's safe to stroll at night.

Banner ads unfold beside my free time like a

cartoon prophylactic. Make a pilgrimage back to the

block where your Flyknits are made. Roll into town,

sweating through a gallery of zapped adolescence

in Bangkok, a trillion times worse than

every guilty cafeteria on the corkboard of your heart.

Good zoning runs interference in the living room,

where Somkid keeps me hot but modest.

A point belabored two ways:

my meticulous summer look,

and his year-long carpal fever.

The story now hides in my jeans with a cache of

other summers I intentionally forget.

Debride the HEATTECH lining

even if it's hiding in my heart. Shear my sneakers

even if I never leave a trace.

I wish I hadn't known that when I'm here I'm family,

since these goggles blush like amber

over the corroborated blue.

No need to say it again. Your worm is your ear;

that is a wonderful thing. It's amazing how

many acres of you can fit inside the world's smallest,

omnipotent object. Buy more clouds to house

the proof; it would hurt too much

to forget you.

In some hasty fantasy everything

has already been fought for. The right to

bring tuna to the breakroom gets in line behind

the chip on your shoulder. Vacation at home.
Rub peanut-butter on a pacifier. Don't read the
news after 8. Each error isn't a bee crashing a
Bonnet or a blemish on the face of a baby.
  Ambassador of hives, see my automatic reply.
   I am 110% with you on every last issue,
     but have limited access to email while my family
         surfs the carpeted curve of our birth canal,
             chilled with cucumber melon.
             Baths and bodies go to work,
       rallying to patch the organic fabric that keeps these
          two weddings separate. In the middle of the night
your name quakes, and you decide you are a saint
   by force of invasion. If there really is only
  one direction, and it is this, just be sure to
     ignore each patented tremor of your life,
affirmed inside your purse during dinner.

          Come back from the wilderness
  with a ragged mattress and a menacing set of Crocs.
The shelf life ruined all life. Same with insurance.

The promise of more sticks out its tongue

and rims the curve of our emergency excess.

You post about the weather and sex work from

a porch swing with excellent lumbar support.

The garden is a metaphor. Feel free not to take it

too seriously tonight when the speed of life

collaborates with its curfew.

If I could put everything on pause,

I'd write about the space between your butt

and whatever comes next. I apologize for

not navigating your life with enough kindness,

or mistaking my self as my birthright.

It's clear now how much I

miscommunicated your beauty.

Late revelations land like

furniture thrown into a pool.

The surface tension just laughs back and eggs you on.

I would have liked the chance to uncast my ballot

if only to say that there was more

I should have said.

You can actually fuck a baby up by being its mother

and talking at a different rhythm. Look,

you are absolutely radiant, but not at

the usual frequencies that cradle me into sequences of

excess and loss, cooing into the recesses you dug

just to saunter back in at your whim. It's killer.

It isn't mine, the site went public, thank god,

but the temptation to beg for a share is bulldozed by

my wish to look effortless. So baby I cruise instead,

spinning figure-eights, flaying in graceful submission

to the Zamboni, and then leaving the rink with

the scent of a public gust. I exit as many;

my scent is the crowd-sourced conclusion of sweat.

The site went public, so I can go home.

I type in the address, try to click beyond the

doorframe. All treasures hide behind curtains of

digital bouncers who don't know my name.

Access denied, my treasure is demoted to

the fact that it never could be treasured at all.

My attempts to enter are redirected into

a growing portrait of increasing blurriness;

the roof of the building is

the Tetris of my wet desperation.

I divide inside the anxiety of having said

too many names, so transparently

stacking blocks into a complementary skyline

that fits perfectly into the negative space of

everything I desire. You

dematerialize inside the name.

How I love to hear it.

I submit to the confection of hypnosis,

hard-sold sweetness parading in loops without seam,

like white noise. It spills out of my iPhone in

democratic frequencies beneath rotating banner ads

that blur every distinguishing detail,

third-degree burns on each and every fingertip.

I crawl into the lap of my pixelated fantasy,

because I cannot enter the house.

I get tossed by a phantom bouncer who relays that

Invasion, Wendy, is something

more violent than the blatant *oursness* of

its Russian translation, ultimately testifying to

the violence of *oursness*,

in which anything that is *ours* is an offense,

in which this was originally *yours*,

in which I am the latecomer, arriving in a public gust

so diligently single-filed behind me that

I had no idea it was there.

One of a kind is really a veiled declaration of plurality,

so heartbreaking in its accidental complacency.

I know you know also this;

I am everyone down there.

To be real, I fucking love this shit.

I was hacked for nine months and I wish I still

vacationed inside the company of

anonymous invasion.

These are the secrets we keep;

precocity expires like the winnings on everything.

I played the slots and got fucked by

the most miserable Eros in the house,

dismissed into the distance with every fallen tree

beyond earshot. I know you also know this.

I return to the crowd-sourced conclusion of

my ghost, to my beloved hacker who spent

nine months inside my name as a kind of "relief,"

because she "knew *of* Wendy,"

but didn't "*know* Wendy,"

and made too many weed-jokes in the AIM chat

to fool Jenny into thinking she *was* Wendy.

Hacker swears she only wishes me the best.

Jenny says, "Huh, hacker, well, we all secretly love you."

It has been so long since I had sex the way I wanted,

except that yesterday I did, only after identifying

the unquestionable ripple, and then submitting to the

fortress of a fluke. I end with a Gettier, in which

stimulation is an accident of my low threshold for

pleasure. The truth is the coincidence of

a fact that gets lucky twice over, in which

a stranger's repetition undermines

the happenstance they walked in with.

"*The* truth" takes a definite article,

but there is no antonym that does the same.

The baby's rhythm is just this,

the negative wager of all it is not,

sucked up into the synthesis of its positive yield.

How many times have I revealed that I went

to boarding school past the expiration of true reveal?

Baby, I was deflated, positively fucked into

the smallness of a prophecy I had maybe

one tenth of a say in making.

The site was hacked, went public, became me.

I did not beg for my share.

My adolescence falls on ears like

the toasted light of 4 p.m. in a jump cut to

faded pre-teens splashing crushes in a lake,

like that half-second shot of what you thought was

explicit content, but was just blurriness

around the waist, a shape of baited expectation,

aware of our ability to mistake.

Ghost is just the name I give to indivisible mystery,
too impatient to swallow a nameless gulp.
I cool down in the velvet-lined nomenclature
of agency. My edges are cushioned by all the anthems
I drum up around me. I can't keep the rhythm, baby.
I herald your loss in my off beats.

The fan kicks in and drowns out
every gesture into the commonality of sound.
My white noise deletes me.
The baby lives, and really, it's for the best.
I need others to be me.
I have been a wet leaf swaying listless at the bottom
of a pool. I have been candy embraced by the traction
of asphalt. I regained levity, holy helium,
rising up to the seam between water and air,
breaking up several crowds of algae as I shake off
the weariness I've been lugging for weeks.
Excitation is a gift, a blue moon I spurn to
hunker down to the fabulous anatomy of Work,
which I don't do. In my down time I steal bases

from someone else's diamond, aware of theft as

an abstraction, but never an action

I am capable of performing. *It wasn't me.*

I performed Shaggy twice at karaoke when

she was in town, submitting my vocals to

the honeyed grain of sex on domestic surfaces.

You were once goofy at parties

and now lay flush with the tarmac in anticipation

of greater adversity. I am suspended in the pale

infinity of Epsom salt, senses deprived,

the water ripples with each hiccup

as I wait for an intruder to join me and

banish the murmur from my body.

This won't happen if you are born into every priority,

but cushy fate can have a rumble so violent within

the stomach, that every last drop is displaced

beyond the bathtub.

God of rain, or something way more basic.

I lap up the excess; I steal bases where I can.

I donate my diamonds and gain publicity from

other rinks. I am a dandelion on ice,

spinning circles around the fate of two giants who

wait for me to fall on my head or my tail,

delivering two fortunes at once, reduced to

a tiny unit of currency, spaced out like

the Nickelodeon Jr. trope of logarithmic zoom,

infantilizing *Powers of Ten*,

riffing off of earlier *Cosmic Views*,

delivered in the hot pigment of

animated de-magnification. Flipped,

I donate split destinies without being asked,

ringing around absent roses before I get nailed to

the sun of my absolute verdict.

I was taught to be good,

delivered the bubble-gum back to the counter

upon pocketing its sweetness past the threshold of

a now memorialized bodega.

I promise to be good.

Fire the bouncer and beckon me

beyond the doorframe.

Recognition lands faulty like every textured cannon,
and really, I lay blame so badly.
I lap up the moat around the monster
just to eat myself into a genetic tendency to devour,
absorbed into the manufactured *oursness* of
my domesticated Eros. I steal diamonds just to
cash into the warmth of your doorway.
I get fucked beyond my ability to care.
The rhythm sags because I'm so *over it*,
in which my inability to identify *it* leaves me
rampant within it. This song literally lassoes
and delivers the experience of brimming sweat into
the fabric seats of someone else's car as we
race down the Taconic toward a fabled lake,
just minutes from being demoted to
the height of its reality,
inflated, for these minutes, in the prefatory gleam
of the sweetness delivered by the hook of a different
rhythm, bringing the baby to the edge
and then back again.

And here all I wanted to talk about was that
terrible *n+1* party, coveting an optical illusion
of good attendance, lying flush with the truth
of it being a bust. I lost the whole game
in the bad frequencies I couldn't help but sing while
I was begging to be someone else's relief.
Nine months of multiplicity,
gently mimicking the time it would take
to make us the same.
Bearing the distance, bearing into the distance,
born into the impossibility of creating
anything that is *ours* to fuck up.

The idea of water breaking is so appealing,
as if a liquid were by nature a solid.
This tender conga performs
a pleated asymmetry of gesture,
like massage circles at summer camp.
I receive text messages begging for a response,
and beg others in kind. My +1 does not respond,
and in the negative space of a ghost
I receive every rhythm,
returned to sender.

GAK

If I'm teased for the jellyfish,

I'm teased for the jellyfish.

Joy buggy, hey.

It's crazy how this all turned out.

I still want to write about the white Burmese jeans

and the nape of the temple, National Grid

and Mimolette in the refrigerated glove compartment.

Erica and I never used

our season passes to Catamount in 2011.

I dropped very many things.

That's all. I dropped them.

There are several pictures from that

UNESCO World Heritage town

where I got my period on the comforter,

and Bataille lived,

and one of Bruno eating tripe in his kitchen.

God, Bruno, I really fucking miss you.

I'm sorry I was such a shit in junior year.

Thank you for letting me turn 21 in your living room,

and loving me. The Verizon store didn't

save your voicemails when I upgraded my phone.

You couldn't bear it, but I still don't know what *it* is.

If I take myself to task, this is what I come up with.

Something enormous in Tours,

stored in the infinite chorus of what's to come.

That moment only outwardly arrives,

like the Gak in my hair at Toys "R" Us

or the day Abilify paralyzed my face into smile

while I was crying on the swings at Four Winds.

In your room, I didn't get older,

  but the memory is the face-card,

      face-down on a green fleece table,

       touching the fertile cursor of

         your sweet inverted eve.

        I call you calling me in the morning.

      The grammar of noon looks

       deliberate on your face.

MAXIMUM MAY

It's May.

Cubes of memory foam hug Jenny

when she falls off the high beam, arriving by

midday in Houston in a single, legible momentum,

while my heart shakes, the house flips a few times

and I could have died when I was in the air,

but felt OK then,

as the return ticket didn't specify

what would be waiting at the heart of point A,

you, homesick in 2013,

baby's first anaphasic splash in the blind spot of

a blessed twelve-year-old's nap time,

making June waves, OK, I won't leave myself

anywhere that could activate fast relapse on a

different kind of drive in which I still could have died,

but felt OK,

so long as you know to bury me

beneath the snow in California,

and return me to the posture of objects

in coarse, topographical attachment

to amenable Eros and passive consent,

since speech is a limited resource,

and worse on behalf of what isn't,

a ghost in the listening kingdom,

sat chatting at the counter with a milkshake

while, away now, your bed sulks, and all I can do is

cry in line for the bathroom or miss you more and

less than is meant by a single secondary address,

leaving Saturday to someone else's bedside,

outing every sky that still relies on

the straightness of our gaze,

while Roadrunner drops

before we even leave the runway.

Dearest pound coin.

You've already happened.

A heads up is all you would need on a day like this,

when sickness is a lamp you lowered in the morning

and forgot by night, a rashy mosaic of

dying many times. The landlord stays back

from Burning Man to watch the dogs

and offers me Rohypnol on the porch.

That was a while ago. Oakland never gets cold.

In Cyprus you realize that

the only way to beat the arrhythmia of rain

is to play *SimplyRain* on loop

with the seam turned out,

like the hem on the tip of your socks.

Blue air angels do flips right above us. Chutes of

mild curiosity show like leaf bugs in the desert.

In the ripstop parachute of the day,

we find a way to get wet without breaking the egg.

You go blond in front of a hardwood McDonalds

and I really miss you, as Cuba gets eaten like

a superfood on midnight release.

Somehow it still feels good,

ghosting this 69 galaxy loop-track,

like a circular hug, or thumb sucked in public

against the adumbrated wonder.

A terrarium of night terrors fills out the house,

like a bad party. In the food court, girls dance in

postictal shakedown to Noah's attenuated raven,

breaking up sequences of pollen and guilt.

You go home, knowing the soft-palate will

eventually depress, redistribute, and bless you.

After dinner we pull out the baby pics.

I began blonde with almond eyes.

People are coming home for Christmas;

I'm not supposed to call them.

But I still love you,

even when the world hurts, and the

very realness of this feeling relieves the need to

dig deeper, as the shovel becomes a Q-tip that

might make you deaf, but won't ever leave you dead,

face down in Mexico City with an ice pick in the back.

Something horrible gets caught on repeat.

I can't be more specific.

I tell Kitty I love her daily,

even if it means I forget to march.

I've always staged this unnecessary election

and picked Dukakis on fire.

In the final episode

we can't choose between each other's lap or the world,

since you can't see the world with your head

in a lap, and your lap is just legs

without someone's head in it.

WAVES

≈

Unplugged beside the evacuated sea salt you reset, weaning off the elliptical lifetime of April. Today swears off the sum of three hot corners and the gloss of a face you remember some, but not enough of. Come up in the scopic resurrection of a weekend at the beach, still discharging its celebrity months beyond naturalized comfort. Come down inside the bed. Remedial fruit flies swipe right by the shoulder of what meaning you can currently afford. Next year will account for the difference. At some point, coincidence triumphs, evicting a hypothesis of cause that stayed too long, unwelcome in your apartment. The cats give a rash; the gift basket does not ask you to come back. But the plush revival underwear inherits the mood inside the room, and your heart, mimicking the inability to wake up different every day, as if all things being equal, no thing could ever compare. I study your face, which is vulgar and sweet, like the irreducible mystery of Cool Whip. You are there and yet not at your disposal. The catheter redirects our epic to a park where a secret forensic tenderness overestimates the integrity of lunch. We succeed at the speed of decency, which is the best way to have and give it. There are several things you and I spy; the stranger's fake ID is the most westerly coordinate of pleasure. Every key is a double invagination of floor-space and ordinary goodness. Recycle the entrepreneurial freeze. Get swept away by your life in miniature. The dioramic East Coast is waiting for your little world to board, propelled by the jet-stream of bagels. Like your mother and the sun, you will either die or be absolutely fine. Let hoverboards fly again. Make America weep. The air above the flame waves you in, like the approximate equality of August. Some day, someone will remember us pregnant with two twin squiggles in reciprocal piggy-back, flying in the erotic lockstep of dolphins. The invitation in fall is an ornament to the recourse of fun. It brings you back.

≈ ≈

Decals of love spit up the dial-tone like nylon prayer flags. You constitute at least one remaining stanza of attachment, putting the lyric on pause with the ethical bedrock of debt. It's nothing to be ashamed of. Her legs upset you, over and over again – a smooth olive tonic on the way to what you can't touch. I tried you back and got nothing but net-worth; your mattress filled with Camembert. I am perfectly turned on and shut down by the repulsive taste of cream. For instance: your thigh rips open the seminal juice box, splashing face-paint on the taboo of incest and sending my prize to the waiting room. Evening collects in the plexiglass as the room somehow ricochets your mood. There is a line that can't be walked. From the streets to my desk, where I saved your iridescent headshots in a set. A menagerie of chopsticks tests the tenderness of stakes not drawn to scale. It's exactly what it looks like: most days I imagine myself wrapped around my mother's ankle, or one of several lesser proxies. Dreams down pay the balance of what can't be staged in life, where I imagine the force of synthesis to be stoppable by a single disposable contact lens, placed on the tip of a penis. Yours or mine; we keep switching places. How else to felonize the scoliosis of class, or have uncommon consequence in a zero-fault state? Very little happened in the time it took to pass from conditions of rain to snow. The sky opened up and watched us waste the day. A barely reflective stretch of cellophane takes our wavy portrait, but can't remember anything. It is exactly what it looks like. Our non-negotiables are comfort and an endlessly replicable nursery.

≈ ≈ ≈

Crushed particulars line up between your face and its reflection, meeting the binary siren of your nostrils. In a wood booth we do it. Lay down a baggy analogy of tragedy and lap up the powdered remains. You reject the dualist premise from your disconnected keppie in defense against the pain that lays you down, narrowly able to do anything but look another way. A wave of shame meets the bank of your face. Our apocryphal trauma lays code inside the bunker. Facts peel off the cue-card in the heat of a weakened agreement, where the catheter directs our epic to the bed. It's weird to see you in uniform, doing laps around the floor and dozing off. If it's what's on the inside that counts, then why keep saying it? And if time is just the bad math of popular opinion, then why does it hurt you to move? The circumference of recovery descends around your belly, like an inflatable tube in the Hudson. I swap my head for your tongue and your storge for my optimistic forecast: our future is clear blue ultra and the furthest thing away from the frame. It looks good from here, where the hills of the desktop are your body's natural curves. The feelings don't really go away. That's just the undertaste of age, inaugurating its laws in the heat. No more clues. No matter how pink, the limit case is inevitably your bellybutton. The insides eject a new message: tonight, we drink lemonade and do everything twice.

THREE SEASONS

HORSES

I start to crash in the night. Arriving by fire on
the curved-out balance of replay, down-paid by the

manger. That horse I rode, that horse I fell off, that
horse I ate out of disbelief in the myth of pelvic

deafness. Girl with more than one pearl. Each knee
represents an archive of live feeds copied on carbon

for keeping. Weakened by striated playdates where
sex makes nascent waists of the state we are waiting

to break. Fell forward. Heard back. Figs and phones
make stores of moisture in the armory. A soggy

democracy of objects, none responsible for the rain
that rings out like siblings in the dative case, a lateral

horizon of crowns on your reproductive matrix. The
statue remains untouched, negatively stating the

restraint that makes it so. Every weakened dream
evacuates the capital. Undone by the rent of life on

property, eggs sucked through an extra-vaginal straw
at the office. Pundits wonder, the unwinnable fertility

of a future in which two exits enter into the other,
swaddling the stage in glue and fruit, walking

blocks of bottom confidence. That birdsong was
wrongly accused of grammar. Escaping to your name,

inaudible to the palm trees and weeks of needy
reason. The time-share's childlike riddle of finding

two moms locked into a single refrain. I do not
operate in the morning. Each instance is inoperably

full of the rest. We meet in a new scene of reading
where dawns of disco reflect the one true imposter

of equestrian sovereignty in the carotid body of water.
That gallop is you. Paced out by the dated desire of

continental breakfast and friendship. Slipped disk in
the midst of your blessing. Not one, but an un-

disclosed multitude of bandanas wrapped on shacks
of matted fur for keeping. Hoops of oversized elastic

strap on the Olympic épicerie. You stick the needle in
my thigh with fruit and pancakes, reenacting the

worst of our best arrested keppie. What goes on down
there, between two balding palms without a tree? The

supple science of a sweet, indentured future, where a
gesture systemically melts you. A life puddles up,

running not from cops or faucets, but the freaked-out
temperature of events not yet ready for view.

Educating the real unfettered ghost clone, a hole to which
you happily retire beside the twice bypassed

pinks and curtains of delicate circulation. Paused on all
fours before us, buoyed by confusion, flicking switches

of squinted recognition; the egg undoes the order
of operations, so the incident begins at least twice.

What is it that sends the left-aligned message out of pressure, rigged-up to a twisted furtive pulley so that the bedroom extends to the weather? Our snack municipality is sweet and plainly impossible. No, you cannot come back to assist with the original fish shack if your sequel inexplicably fails. The oil gets too deep in the once abandoned boar's hair. You are stranded in the anonymity of center-city where the incidence of franchise approximates a public. Suspended by the myth of rocks but not objects, the level expels its air in the privacy of a silent drumbeat. Diminishing returns from the bridge that dissolves as you walk on it. Leaves leave leaves in the mouth as light disappears into the spooky looping music of the swampy opposite bank. Learning love on dummies is the ruse of all workable substitutions. Cells get wet, left on burlap chests. No, you cannot get back into the same bed you left. The real non-transferable ticket is you. Aboard this cruise by diachronic loophole, you swear by the rate of exchange and the temperature of customary dress. Tagged by speed and free play in this famously unbeatable level, we sub out. I am standing with my arms behind me. I am here, refreshing the double-bound complaint from a villa within. I am very inside. You are more than one way out. You are the coordinates of a clue to the obsessive, Vitruvian escape room. You are the indecipherable grin on tour, cum foil to all predicted ratios. Heavy metals divine the retirement of all runners up. In place of you, nothing. There would just have to be more.

The water reflects everything but the fish, fidgeting. Whose axis spins on the same index finger, whose ingress deletes the actual arcade. Possibility lays flayed before our separate reservations as range-of-motion invites the body to corroborate. The authenticity of mucus reliably anticipates the arrival of that guest on all fours. She hangs back beneath the glass with two unfocused knees and thirty squirrels. The light switches into our armpits, showing rose gold plateaus of a secret sensitivity and a rapidly dilated subject. Night dissolves the panoramic visor and peals back a view. Now you see it. Now you kill the mystery between your belly and everything else. Blessed by cardinal direction, stilling all Four Winds as they threaten to impress on the incident. Got caught on deck with pickled peppers and sex, escaping nation and heat, losing track of our limits in generous embellishments of night. Imagining that proximity pleased me. Gave grammar to the mountain in bursts of retrospective thirst. I can't tell what the rivulets of impossibly soft access are saying, but I get the message. You kneel down, leveling with busy signals embalmed in citronella. There's a password for the party: it's the crevice where histamine brings your body into knowledge. We still don't know exactly how the roads work, but it's okay. Soon we'll be full of the ocean, unburdened by borders in the flood of two canals not wanting for the opposite.

FOUR QUESTIONS

Too fond of the things I've been taught to be fond of. Kind to bees and dogs off leash, an unnecessary custodian of the animals that surround, high, divided, wrong every time, towing the insensate center toward the poverty of its original cause: that sex is how you got here and why you will eventually leave, having remained technically aware but functionally blind in the meantime for want of a different desire unknown to the documented tastes of home and safety, ready and edible to the crowd that surrounds, alligators unable to give love but radiating a name you insatiably accept, as if it were good to take care of that imaginary life, or the resident consensus to whom it belongs, ignoring yours, clearing debris from a body of shame in which the legs will inevitably give out, leaving you to say "yes" to the resident angel who asks if you are drowning off the coast of your responsibly buoyant home, vomiting gold mesh amenities that can't hold your sequin dream as you wake up screaming, soaked through the unzipped cotton hoody placed beneath your waist that belatedly refuses to save you as waste makes its way to the mnemonic bottom of the mattress, releasing your formerly invisible crush, now documented in the sheets, insisting on saving the life that remains as you continue to toss in only one of two ways so that each cheek expires, vacations, and returns to work on the double-sided face of a confession not yet ready to be made, promising to vacate the excess it holds by itself, mimicking the seasonal storage of fruits, hoarding the impossibly forested future like squirrels gone wild while arresting the wrong side of the sidewalk, bringing good lives to ground in the miscarried tragedy of bad recognition, missing your face for the trees that hold secrets in canopies of 3-D leaves as we seek unseen immunity and idols beneath the least most-populated plaza where gravel remembers the skin of your cheek, and the depression of rocks is a mnemonic, lost as soon as we walk, commuting across those same streets among others unable to breathe, rolling through the space that remains of a not-so-distant cloud on the verge of maxing out, filled with variations of ordinary sunsets and faces too intimate for deletion, rising to the brim of its ability, unable to save anything beyond what it already contains, failing to testify to the face of this loss, dying of heat but unable to join the hotspot as a moment of life or death is forgotten off-screen, intentionally or accidentally ignoring the breach of a historical border between the secrecy of heat and the cold hostility of the street against which you feel each of your cheeks let go of the fruits that you keep, dying for a love you can't reach, too intimate to be deleted or freed, screaming in your sleep, meeting your brim and then receding, intentionally or accidentally forgetting to speak or remember the rest of you, as you rest very far from peace.

The key to the allegorical form is a basement in Alabama. Robbed of topsoil. Nothing grows in these gray zones where the party is a paralyzed flash mob in shrapnel, or glitter, wishful fictions of renaming the playground, but deep down you know that language was never actuarial. Call to get a quote. Call the super who moved us to blow beauty and brains all over the supply chain. Made fresh daily, this hesitant declension of flowers captures something inexchangeable in the trade route. Skies imply the absence of aluminum so the users return in twos. When the last joint is fused, no knees remain to pray on. But they prey on impulse and riddle and error. Pray to god and robotics and insolvency. These new birds can memorize the address, reciting the bushes in evidentiary backstroke. Zoom in to find scribbles in the window saying "death to executive realism, this efficiency is killing too efficiently." Each day is crowded and lonely, coagulating into atoms instead of a real bloc or body, an indivisible slab of granite on the island. Interspersed behind the columns is a hyphenated blind spot. When you least expect it, the shadows assemble into nighttime. Inside is an isolating colony of hell, so described by the one who confided in the operator. He repeats the welcome line in crisis saying: Hi, it's Chris from loss prevention, calling to prevent this loss, the operator unable to solve a snowfall that started so long ago. Calls come in from Lebanon, confusing the continents. The line says my friend is collapsing like boxes in the brutally wet desert behind cardboard cut-outs of real horizons and representations of daylight. There is nothing neutral in a place-name, but the gruesome confusion of nursery rhymes take the reindeer way too seriously. From the inside, you see no snow atop the mountains, but a suspiciously milky run-off feeds these higher wait times, putting pressure on the weather to remit to this standard of service and delivery and debt. Compulsively googling running shoes, sending wishes in the universe, not as truth, but a carefully translated message, confessed only to stamp out the appetite. Ashamed to stow that shame away. Call back a call center in Texas to say you never got the message; log a complaint that the box never came. Jason says the scooter is yours for free, so you are free to ride around the joint anarchic birthday as the renegade you claim to be. Jason is killed by a chorus of complaints made in office, wrought in local rock as a monument to a very big mistake. Now you have to repay. Now you have to repent and repay and love him. But nothing too difficult this time. It is too much to tune in all the time. Blow up the dune buggy. Let the piñata leak stocks and options onto the confections collected in its belly. In real time, in another frame, the coin-purse burst its urine all over the runway. Her shimmering initials spell out the boundaries of a carapace in heat. Each element cries out the same, but these ballads are neutralized in unison, sung in rounds to form an insular melodic plot point that vocalizes its goal, and then dies. Prime time whistles between the wind chimes. Some tall order has slipped beneath the cracks of a strike to find your wish in a tinted fulfillment. The trail was never so honestly blazed. Boxes and boxes and boxes are blocking the way. Bleached urchins leach toxins in the office, balloons of too much future just burst into the uniform. You peed in your pants. You spilled magic all over the balance sheet. The unseasonal breeze is drying alibis for down-time in the break room. Ragged hands crowded 'round the refund, saying grace for different destinations. Each arrival discloses the story of its origin. Every delivery bruises its escape route. Reach out to touch the box but leave no trace. There are still no solutions to waiting, but the future is a fruit with many names. A package came for you. It was grazed by amber showers for the fourth time today. In that sense, they came for you, too.

In the garden, privacy collides with wine and Scrabble as I contemplate the single, silicone dome they emptied on the belt at security. How to keep this in perspective, myself, inadmissible to that love or what happens on each side of the border? I find it absolutely intolerable to be made to leave the room. Sex and cat toys punctuate the open-concept honesty of first nights at sea with the fluency of decoys that don't get homesick. I got lonely, went to church, entered a concept hospital for only hair and nails. Zionskirche falls in and out of relation, but only as long as you think it: that this can and can't go on forever, that you do and don't want this to go on forever, that you are safe on planes, in a bathroom, captive, asleep, but that it is better to be out, beyond the idea of your secret interior. I squeezed my thighs tight so I wouldn't fall off. Like most protests, the bruise will drain and then return to stasis. Your dreams turn sweet and then uncomfortably sour as sudden death drafts two teams of unequal need. You are slight and resonant. Your twin leaves the party before you can do the same. Come outside, bearing the shape of the house that you came from. Arrive at the diner, rarified by light-years of desire. Volumes of moss will roll out, red hot along the lava beside the road. Skies divide, the bed dissolves like Dippin' Dots. There is a secret you don't yet know how to confess. The game cannot end in a tie, but you are paralyzed by choice, and terrified by the loss of every side.

TRADE SECRETS

STEEP RAVINE

Anemones incriminated on rock
Respond shyly to fingers in the socket,
Suggesting the face is just an expression,
Or else daylight hits different below water.
If water were a condition of rock and
Not the other way around, our jagged
Avenue of differently shaped lanes
Would swallow both ends of the rubber
Spaghetti, clutched sensibly between two
Opposing instincts that both kill the cat.
Sand keeps the time between your hips,
At which point I open them up in order
To come back, the day after the day
After tomorrow. If months were days.
If the birdsong were spelled out
Phonetically, I would come back
Home and cut the first slices small,
Knowing that cake is just as fickle
In size as states. For instance, we
Had no way of knowing the shape
Of California before we got there.

TOUCH TUNNEL

Beneath the treatment reads a plot

For teenage sovereignty, embossed

On hallways in courtesy of content,

The popsicle sized honesty is the

Practical width of the incident,

Which expands below the doctor's

Palm in the recap. I know exactly

What you mean. We can't hear it.

Until the accent drops, our year is

But a three-week fever in combustible

Linen. The picture fills out with a

Mosaic of smaller photos. Bright

Ones become sun, and the same

Dim interior rims the perimeter of

Two sets of eyes playing hand games

In a hot tub. We inherit everything.

Our meekness wrapped like bacon

'Round the dated earth. For you, for

The guests who round us out, the scene

Is studied in less precision than its

Memory plays back in muscle. Maybe

More, but exactly no less. Is the

Emphasis mine or the event itself.

DOUBLE LIFE

What makes the bedspring laugh
Is our appetite. Shoots of pee
Adorn the porcelain import,
Blushing with each closer approach.
I stayed for years and loved it.
I didn't ever want to leave. The
Guestbook is etched in pencil
On your forearm, plugging the jets of
A jacuzzi. And when, allergic to
Half the house, the pick of this
Un-umbilical litter runs windward,
It will find the fish. We sleep on
Rafts. We choose safety in the
Middle of the night when the world
Combines too coarsely with pubes.
At the mouth of the tunnel, the river
Convenes a public in which our
Specific presence is irrelevant. But
The risk of eviction affirms the

Reverse. That the bed is still ours.

And that it buckles between a unique

Set of forensic edges that lays its

Claim for life. Even when we're up.

Some days will not relent against the
Hesitance of our initial offering. It is not
Uncommon to hang two mirrors across
A hall to see the wave of your hair, or an
Endlessly attenuated legacy. When the
Song stopped, I patented that aspect. The
Knock-offs now cut diamonds instead of
Circles from the approximated Croc. To
Stop the transfer of poppies from one
Prop to another, to inherit your initials as
Peace talks. The family is a stock. To persist
And expire inside the play is a wonderful
Thought. To be a bunch of worms, or an
Acre, hidden plots all around, not to talk
As all of us at once, or as one, or at all.

HEDERA

In the kitchen we realize that
Action progresses only by accident.
Rooms change with the arrival of ivy,
More times than can squeeze between
The record. These inhalations were never
Let out or expressed or represented in size.
When salt turns to looks, and love gets
Lost at sea through the scandal of a peephole,
You look back to ask *Wot ya lookin' at?*
Our plots align by weight class and
The consonance of crawl space.
For decades the UK mistakenly believed
The vines antagonized the trees,
Implying a hierarchy of size. Now,
In this weird, denuded universe,
we will pay for this disinvitation, for life.

ACKNOWLEDGMENTS

Thank you to Dan Machlin and Aiden Farrell at Futurepoem, as well as Hannah Black, Mónica de la Torre, and Ken Chen for making this book possible. Several poems have been published elsewhere. Earlier versions of the poems in "Intense Holiday" were published in a chapbook of the same name by After Hours LTD in 2016. "In the Flowers of Young Girls in Shadow" was published by *BOMB*; "Steep Ravine," "Talk of the Town," and "Prime" were published by the *Chicago Review*; "Pearl" was published by the *Poetry Foundation*; "Foil" was published as a broadside by Arrow as Arrow; "Gliders" was published by *Not for Resale*; and "≈," "≈≈," and "≈≈≈" were published by *Poor Claudia*. Thank you, everyone, for your support.

This first edition, first printing, includes 26 limited edition copies signed by the author and lettered a-z.